COLOR BY NOTE

another nifty notespeller

by SHARON KAPLAN

Book Two

EL 03399

Editor: Carole Flatau
Model: Cathy Priz
Photographer: Warren Conway

COLOR BY NOTE

Book Two

NOTE

another nifty notespeller

by SHARON KAPLAN

CONTENTS

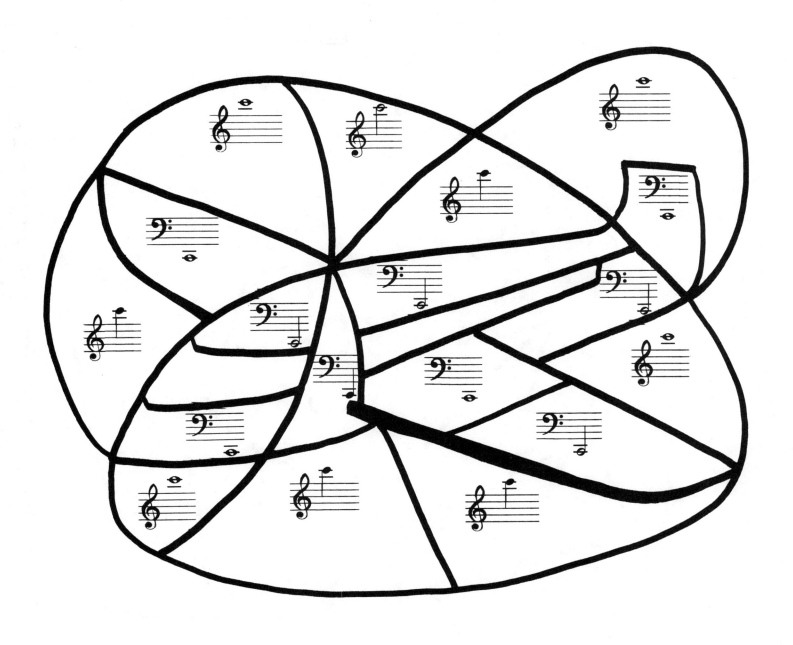

COLOR High C - blue
Low C - silver

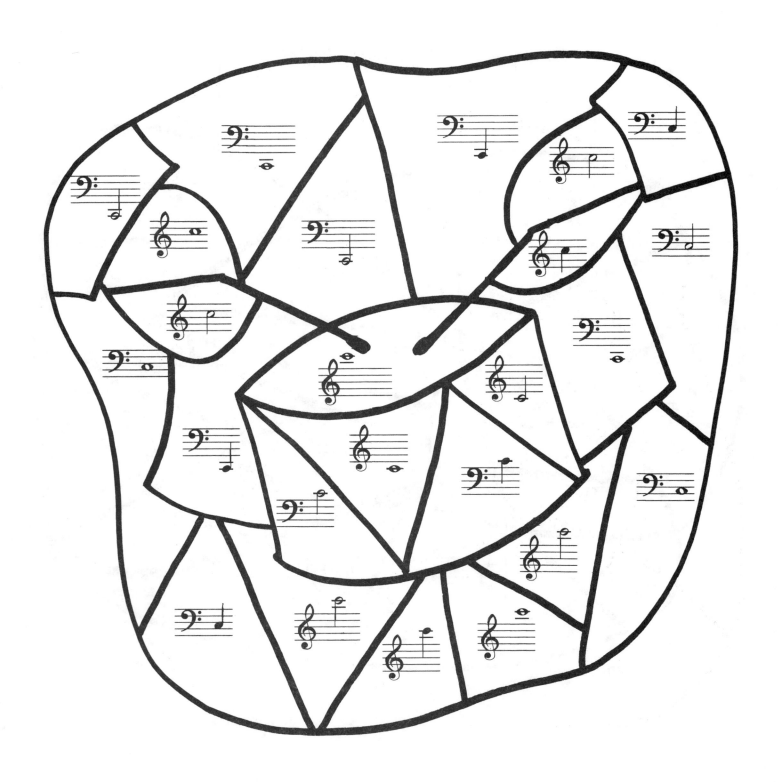

COLOR High   C - white
Treble C - pink
Middle C - red
Bass   C - purple
Low   C - blue

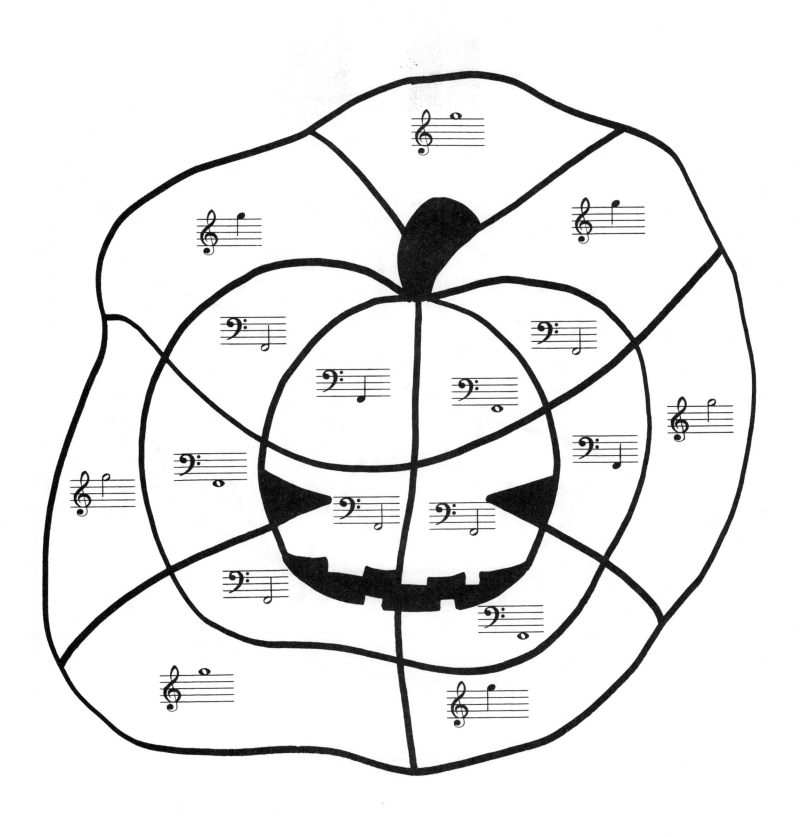

COLOR F - orange
G - purple

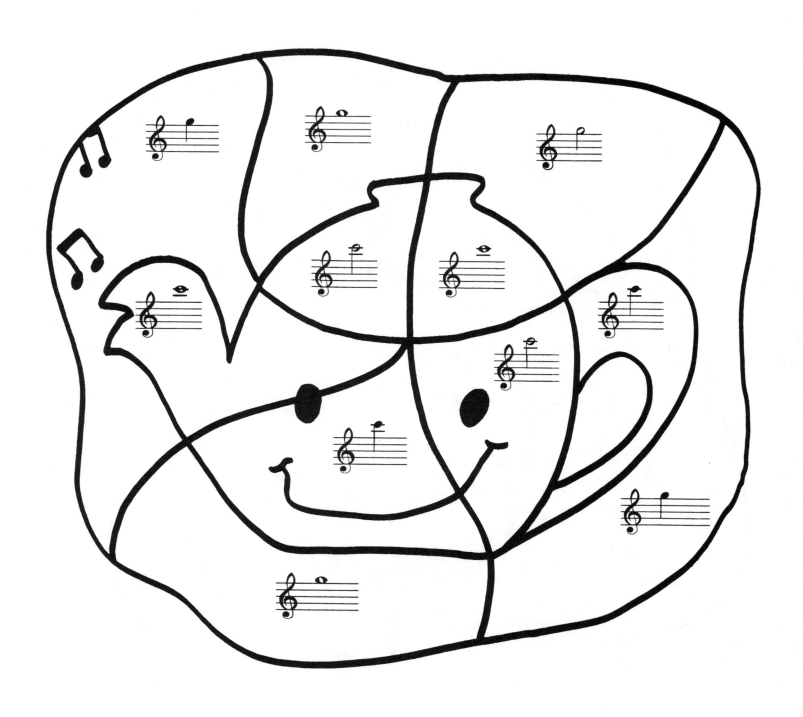

COLOR   C - yellow
           G - green

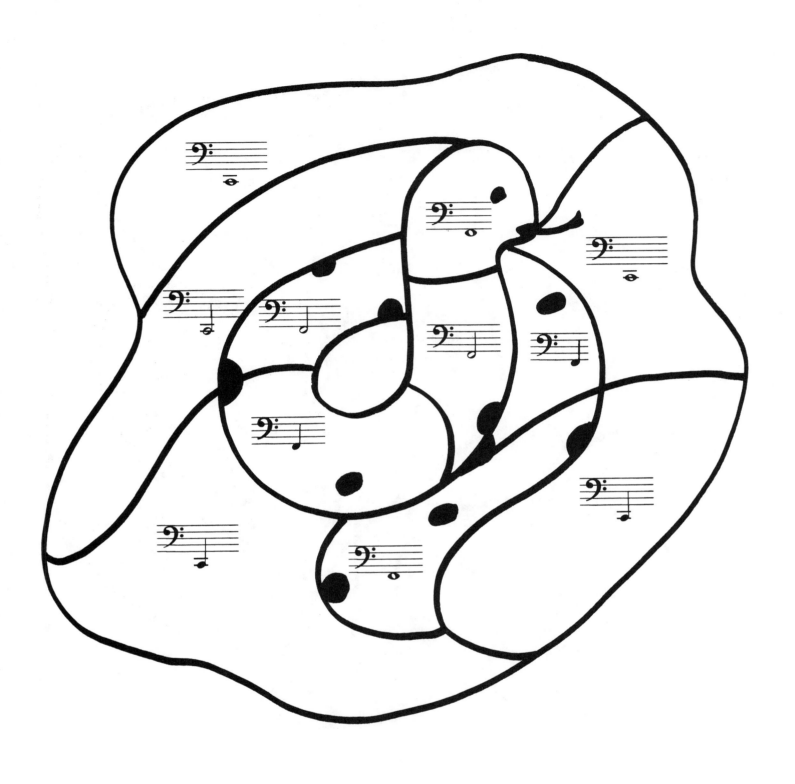

COLOR F - light brown
C - green

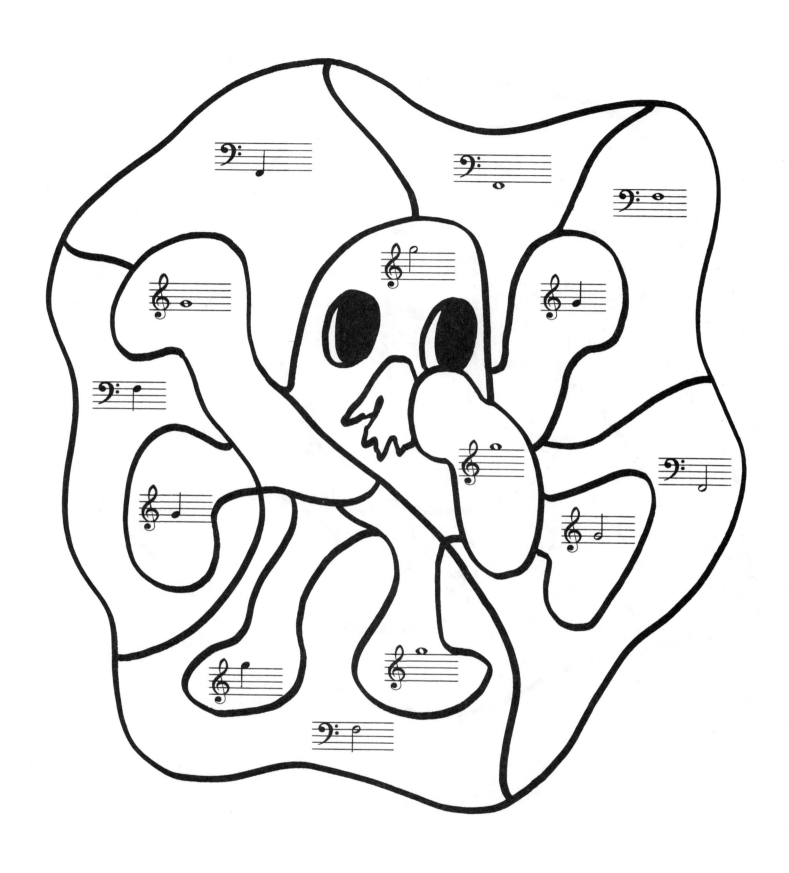

COLOR F - blue

G - gray

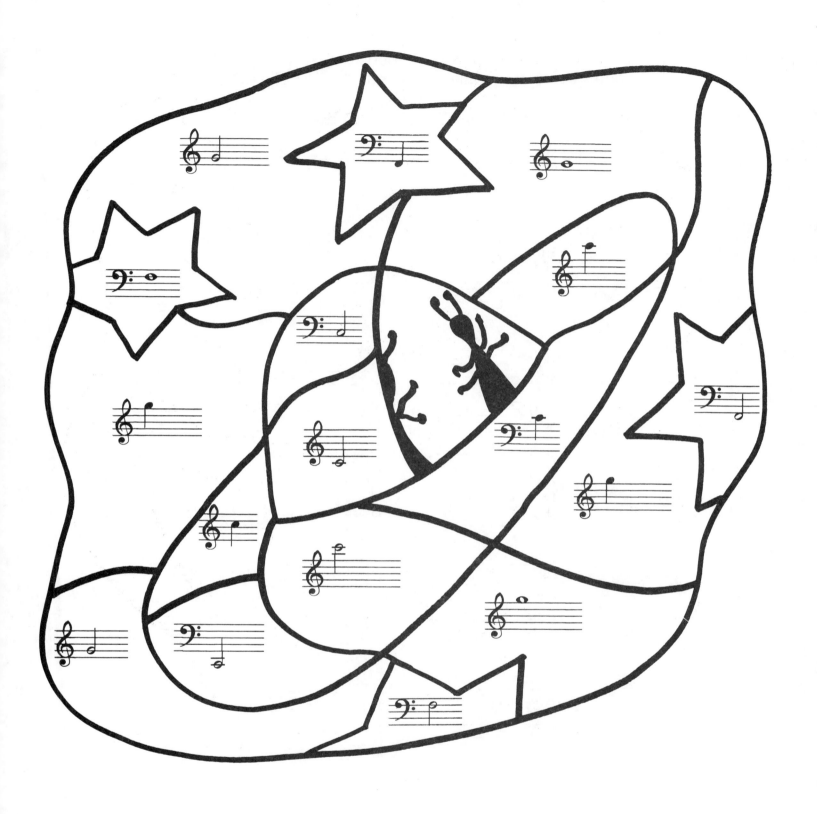

COLOR C - light blue
F - yellow
G - purple

9

HOW QUICKLY CAN YOU PLAY THESE NOTES?

Point to these notes, or have someone point to them for you, in mixed-up order. You're pretty good if you can play 10 of them in 30 seconds. If you can play 10 notes correctly in 25 seconds, you're very good. If you can play 10 notes correctly in only 20 seconds, **YOU'RE TERRIFIC!**

How many times can you be TERRIFIC this week?

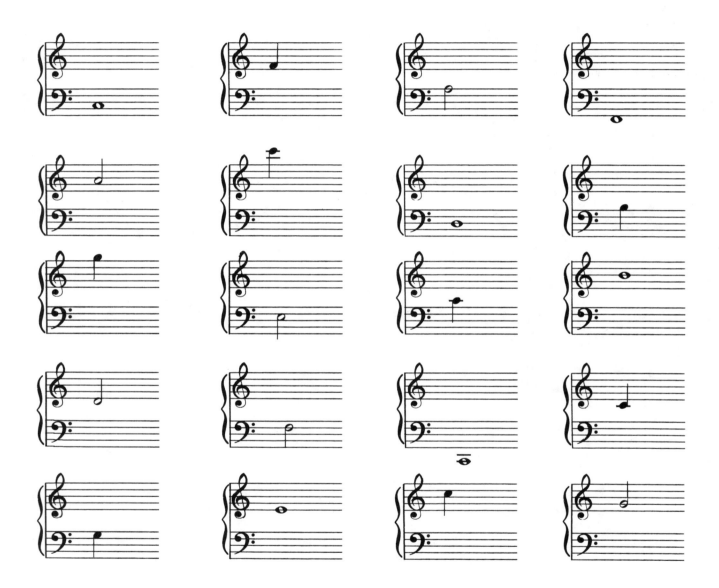

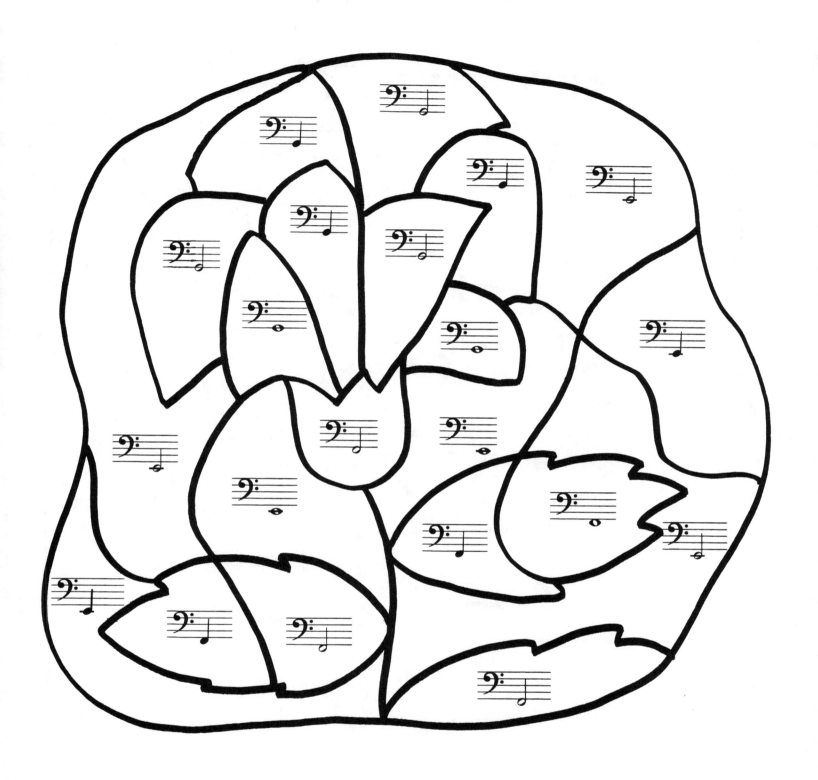

COLOR Low   E - blue
             Low   F - green
             Low   G - red

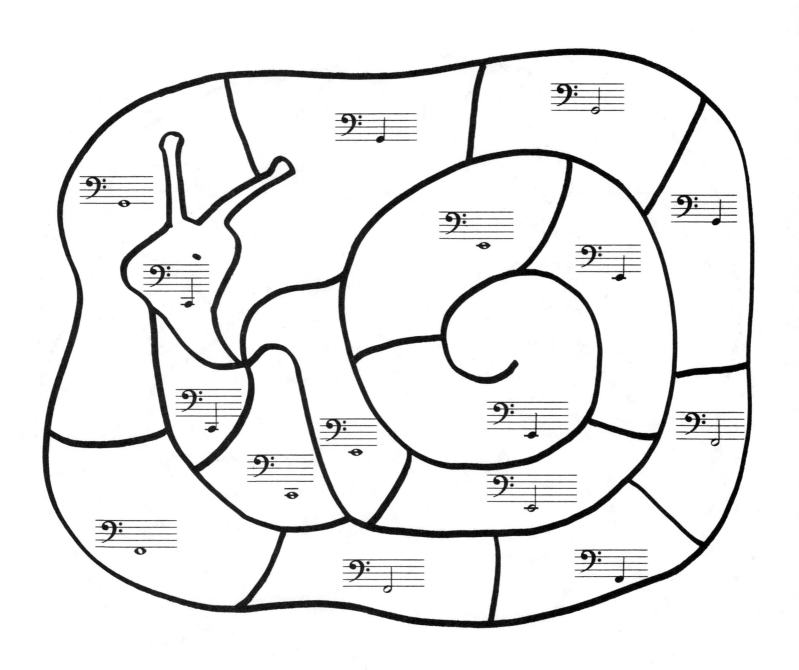

COLOR   Low   C - pink
            Low   E - gray
            Low   F - green
            Low   G - blue

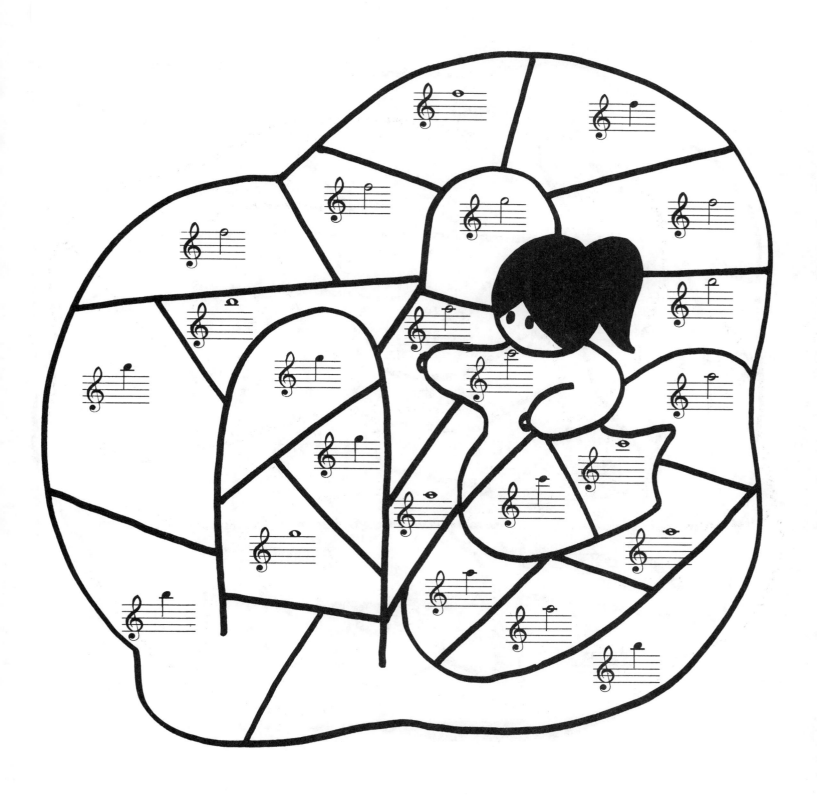

COLOR F - dark green
G - brown
A - yellow
B - light green
C - pink

21

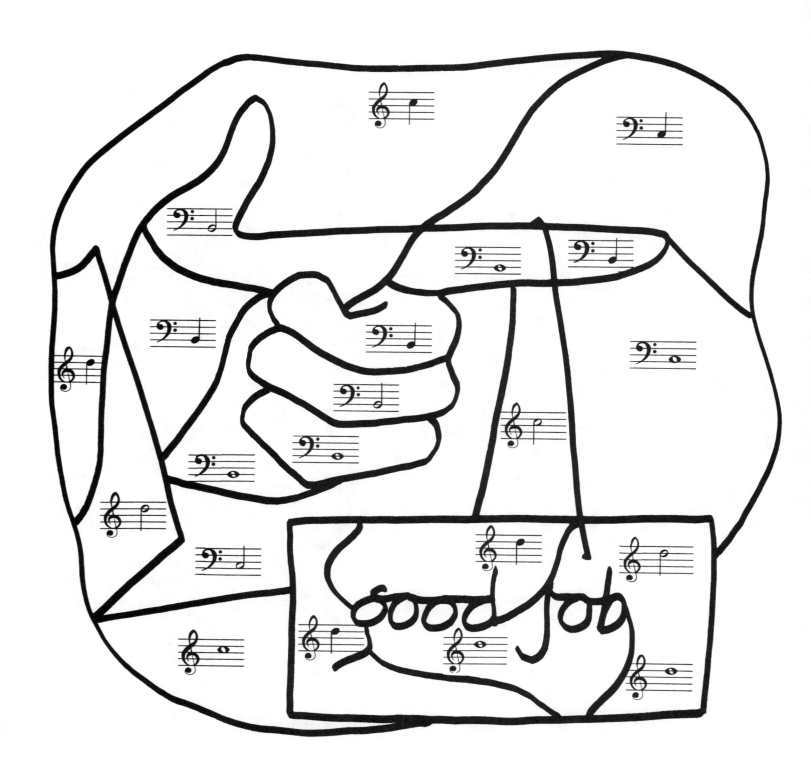

COLOR   B - pink
        C - lavender
        D - light blue

22

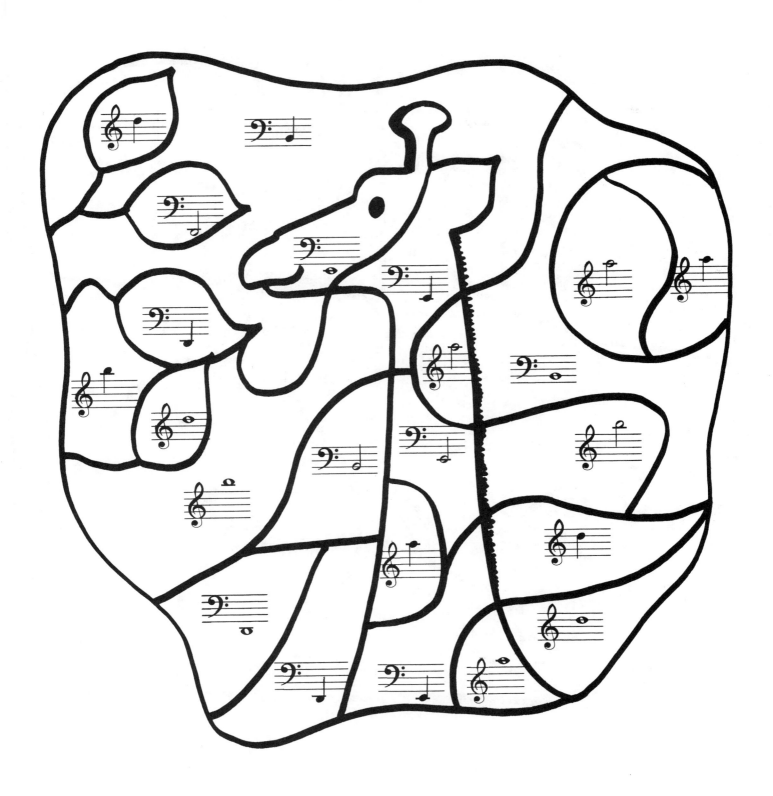

COLOR   D - green
            E - brown
            A - orange
            B - blue

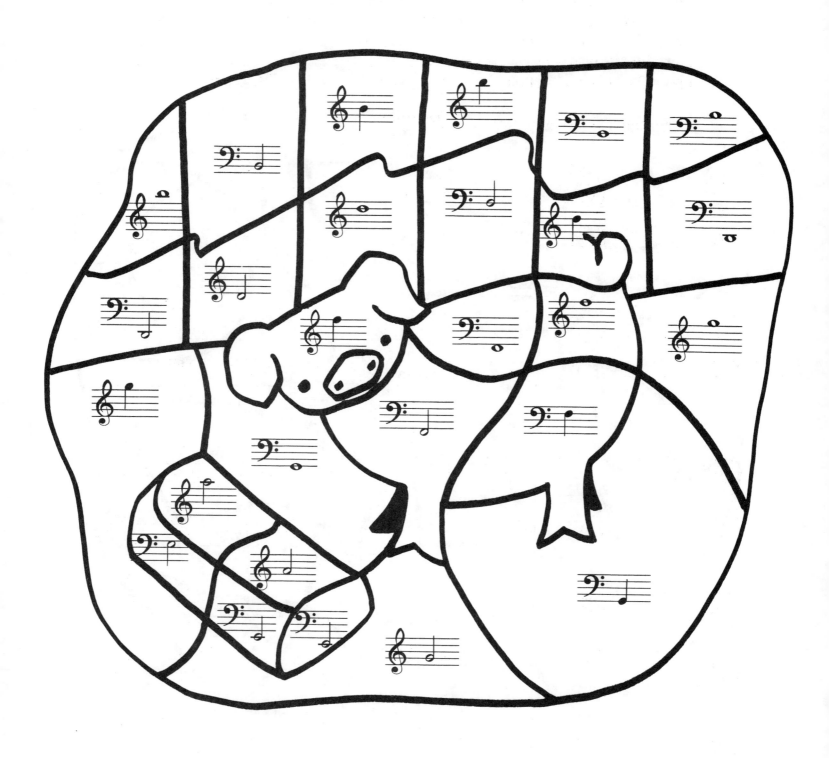

COLOR   D - red
             E - brown
             F - pink
             G - gray
             A - yellow
             B - red orange

HOW QUICKLY CAN YOU PLAY THESE NOTES?

Point to these notes, or have someone point to them for you, in mixed-up order. You're pretty good if you can play 10 of them in 30 seconds. If you can play 10 notes correctly in 25 seconds, you're very good. If you can play 10 notes correctly in only 20 seconds, **YOU'RE TERRIFIC!**

How many times can you be TERRIFIC this week?

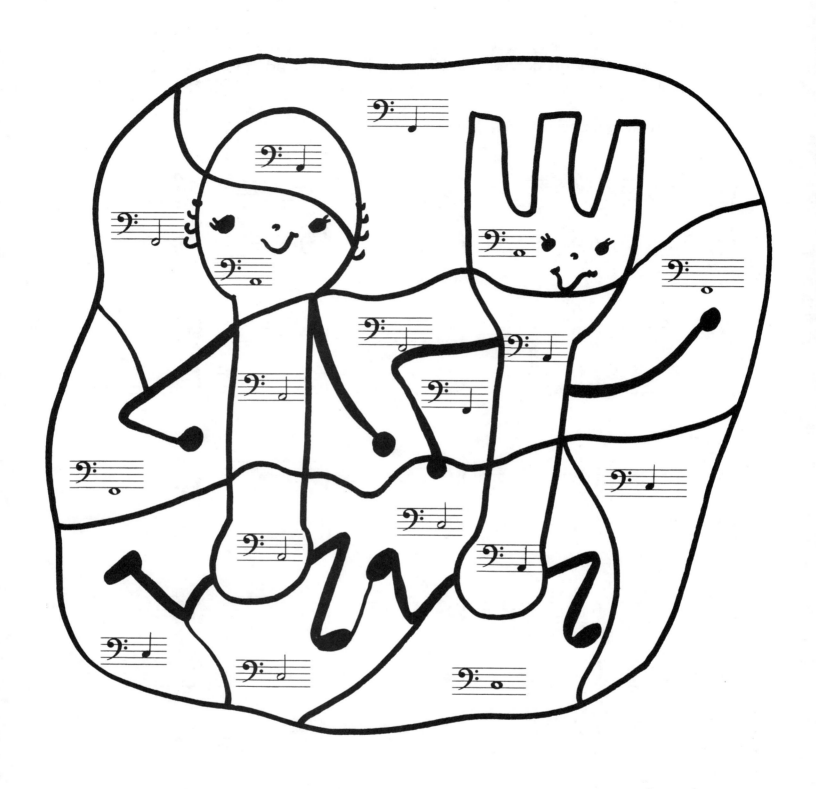

COLOR F - blue
       A - silver
       C - green

26

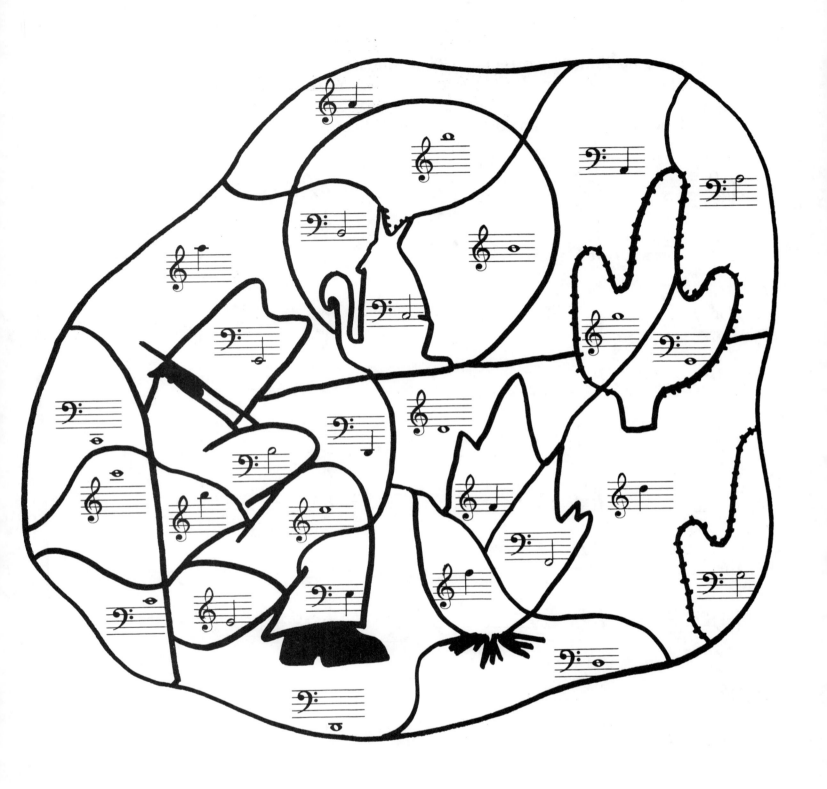

COLOR A - black
B - white
C - gray
D - tan
E - brown
F - red
G - green

HOW QUICKLY CAN YOU PLAY THESE NOTES?

Point to these notes, or have someone point to them for you, in mixed-up order. You're pretty good if you can play 10 of them in 30 seconds. If you can play 10 notes correctly in 25 seconds, you're very good. If you can play 10 notes correctly in only 20 seconds, **YOU'RE TERRIFIC!**

How many times can you be TERRIFIC this week?